The Art of
Strategic Non-Action
Learning to go with the flow

David Tuffley

To my beloved Nation of Four
Concordia Domi – Foris Pax

Leading a country is like frying a small fish – Lao Tzu

Published 2011 by Altiora Publications
ISBN-13: 978-1467928533 ISBN-10: 1467928534

About the Author

David Tuffley PhD is a Lecturer at Griffith University in Australia where he lectures in Philosophy. David is passionate about helping people to self-actualize by learning how to achieve their full potential as a human being.

Acknowledgements

I acknowledge the hundreds of mentors in my life who have shaped this work, which has been in progress since 1970.

To my life partner Angela I owe a great debt for the profound wisdom that she innately possesses, and her willingness to share it with me.

Also the *Turrbal* and *Jagera* indigenous peoples, on whose ancestral land I write this book. This ancient continent has a profound story for those who would listen.

Contents

The Art of Strategic Non-Action

Strategic non-action is a powerful yet under-rated method of influencing worldly affairs. In cultures where action is favoured over inaction, like in many western countries, direct action is considered a virtue while inaction is little more than laziness or cowardice. Let us be more subtle and nuanced in our understanding. There is a time for both action and inaction.

Non-action gives access to a deeper intuitive awareness than that gained through action, since knowledge that comes through action is obscured by situation-specific reactions.

Non-action can be understood as an aspect of going with the flow, not resisting the larger forces that govern a world of which you are a small part. Non-action acknowledges that events are governed by the laws of Nature, and it is often best to simply allow those laws to operate and play out in their own time, in their own way. Taking action often amounts to interference which creates its own problems.

Non-action can help us towards our goals by encouraging patience and taking the long-view. Humanistic Psychology says that it is within our reach to create the life we want for ourselves. As we think and believe, so we create our world. This is indeed true, but only up to a point. We can transform our lives in goal fulfilling ways, but the transformation is relatively slow, its progress measured in months and years.

2

Introduction

We know that for every action there is an equal and opposite reaction; at least we know this is true in Physics if we did not sleep through that class in school.

Less recognised is the truth of Newton's Third Law of Physics in human affairs. Just as in the world of inanimate objects, when we do things to people, we get a reaction. This then causes its own reaction, and a pendulum-like cycle is set up. Think of how people and tribes get into feuds with each other. Strategic non-action recognises the danger of this pattern of behavior and offers the only means of avoiding it.

Non-action gives others nothing to react against. The ideas in this book derive from the ancient Chinese concept of *Wu Wei*, as expressed in Lao Tzu's classic *Tao Te Ching**. First published around 2,500 years ago, it is probably the oldest book still in print, a testimony to the force of its message.

Wu Wei literally means *without effort*. It describes natural action that occurs without contrivance or effort. It simply happens. Think of how plants and animals grow, rivers flow and planets orbit. No-one makes them do this, it just happens without effort or control in accordance with the laws of Nature. Such action is what we should strive for, while avoiding the kind of action that causes counter-reactions.

The chapters that follow investigate the ways that *Wu Wei*, or strategic non-action, can be understood and practiced.

* The corresponding chapter number from the Tao Te Ching is shown in brackets at the end of each chapter in this book.

Selflessness

As the world evolves, what was low becomes high, what was in the background comes to the foreground. Every object in the physical world, the world of phenomena, is subject to this law in which it is transformed into its own opposite, and then back again. We live in a dualistic world.

In the natural world, mountains erode to become alluvial silt in the rivers and seas, and then with the passage of time and tectonic movement, what was low becomes a mountain again.

In human affairs, in politics, the party that is in opposition becomes the government, and then returns to opposition when the electorate is tired of them. There is an old saying in politics that governments are not elected, they are defeated. Even when a tyrant seizes control and out-stays the natural course of his tenure, he is always brought down eventually. In human affairs, it is the ego that is the agent of these phenomena. In the case of the tyrant, his ego becomes identified with the country. He *is* the country in microcosm. He honestly believes it is his destiny to be the leader and that no-one else could possibly do it as well as him.

Evolutionary Psychology tells us that the human ego is a survival mechanism, and a very good one at that. It evolved to develop survival strategies in a hostile environment, going back a million years. It categorizes what it encounters as either helpful or harmful to its survival. The ego perceives a world of dualities, of polar opposites. It is correct in doing so, yet often it does not know when to stop categorising, when enough becomes too much.

The ego is especially strengthened and defined by conflict. In the absence of conflict, it will create conflict in order to strengthen itself. Look around at the people in your world, on TV and movies. Everywhere, people's lives consist of one conflict-driven drama after another. They are locked in egoic thinking, dancing to the war-drums that have been beating in the human psyche for a million years. Selflessness is the way to turn down the volume of those war-drums.

Selflessness is about the diminution of ego. Spiritual traditions like Buddhism are clear that the ego is the greatest impediment to spiritual growth through its tendency to become attached to the impermanent things of the world (and that is everything). It is good to remember that given the cyclic nature of change, whatever we lose comes around again later in another form.

As an enlightened person, you will therefore adopt a strategic position in the beginning of putting yourself last and outside. It may seem counter-intuitive, but remember, when something has reached its peak, down is the only direction it can go. Employ a subtle tactical inertness to compel the social environment to counterbalance and bring you forward naturally. Such an approach calls for patience and a long-term view.

Your chances of success are improved because this approach is unlikely to attract opposition or attempts to neutralise your efforts.

Paradoxically, acting without self-interest actually leads to the eventual fulfilment of your goals. People who put their interests last discover that their desires are transformed. It leads to an expanding awareness of the larger realities of life beyond the ego's demands.

As your awareness expands you develop priorities that are aligned intelligently with both the current situation and with the larger influences in the world. With this alignment, the fulfilment of your goals also fulfils the larger goals of society. (7)

Harmony with the evolving world

Anyone who contemplates the world they live in comes to recognize in time that there is an inner pattern to everything in Nature. This inner pattern can be neutrally described as an *Informing Principle*, thus avoiding religious terms like God.

The influence of this Informing Principle organises the natural world into an immensely complex, inter-connected system that is truly wondrous to even glimpse. A person could devote the whole of a long life to studying it and at the end realise they have barely scratched the surface.

The more one contemplates the inter-connectedness of Nature, the more one comes to recognise that there is a common thread running through everything. There appears to be just one Life in Nature, and that this one Life has many forms. All of the life forms of the Biosphere are animated by the same underlying principle. I do not *have* a life, Life has me. The Informing Principle is what the ancient Greeks called *Logos*.

Cells-replicate, crystals grow, societies evolve and galaxies spin, all according to a precise template that lives unseen, within the entity. The informing principle that resides within everything is fully deserving of respect, even reverence. Yet too often it is ignored and disrespected by people who see only the surface appearance of things and thinks that the world is there to be exploited for their own selfish ends. They do not see the inner beauty. They think in terms of utility and monetary value.

Strategic non-action or non-interference is about recognising this sacred Informing Principle in Nature that creates the complex, inter-connected world and somehow makes it work without any apparent effort. It is about aligning one's mind with it and not working at cross purposes, knowing that to do so would be dangerous and ultimately futile.

But we humans are an inventive species, equipped with a creative imagination that has brought us far on the evolutionary path and which constantly tries to find new and better ways of living. Should we try to silence this desire? No, certainly not. There are many process driven activities that we perform in our daily lives, particularly if we work in complex organisations. When we are dealing with artificial systems, there will always be room for improvement.

Perceiving the inner-workings of Nature and applying this knowledge to the design of processes is an excellent philosophy, as the design field of bio-mimicry clearly shows. One has to find a balance between conservatism and progress. In every society, these two exist in a state of dynamic tension. It is remarkable how finely balanced these forces can be. For example, in a country of many millions of voters, the result comes down to a few thousand votes either way to decide who the new government will be. A mere 0.1% of the voters often decide the outcome, as in the 2001 US Presidential elections.

The advice is therefore to take the broadest view. Stand back and observe the macro-trends in society; how your society and the world are evolving. Doing this will help you perceive where the world will be in five or ten or more years and allow you to position yourself with the right skills and resources to proactively take advantage of the situation, but also it will allow you to perceive what it is you should *not* be doing, given the direction things are moving. Maintain a position that is in harmony with the evolutionary forces that gradually evolve your society.

Your influence is subtly exerted through the force of your focussed inner awareness. So it is you often refrain from taking action when to do so would adversely impact the natural evolutionary flow.

As people get older, they tend to settle into accustomed ways of living. But as society evolves, as it surely does, they become increasingly threatened by what they see happening around them. They become nostalgic about the good old days when life was better, even though by almost any objective standard it was worse. As time goes by, they isolate themselves in a bubble of familiar surroundings and feel increasingly anxious about the outside world.

These folk are taking non-action for the wrong reasons. In this situation, observing how the world is evolving and adapting to it is the best course of action. After all, the world is what it is. Wishful thinking will not change it. Being attached to something which is now gone only creates suffering.

Think of a sapling tree growing on a wind-swept hill. Nearby is the sapling's mature parent. When the winter gales blow, the young tree bends. After the storm, it resumes its upright position. But the old tree has become inflexible, unable to bend. One day, it simply breaks and falls over.

Unlike the tree, we humans can decide to remain flexible, at least in our thinking. (29)

Avoid becoming too specialised

To say that humans are not machines sounds too obvious, yet it seems that in today's world, machine-like is how people need to be if they are to operate successfully in highly regulated environments. The human world is becoming more complex with every passing year because there is a tendency in human affairs over time to move from a less complex to a more complex state.

Strategic non-action in this regard begins with the awareness of this trend and the need to counteract the trend by actively seeking to simplify your world. It is about not making things *more* complicated than they need to be to achieve the desired outcome. Resist the temptation to create something complex unless it really needs to be that way.

Ockham's Razor is helpful. Named after the 14th Century English logician and Franciscan friar William of Ockham, the principle says that in seeking an explanation or a solution to a problem, the explanation that involves the fewest assumptions is likely to be the best one. In other words, the simplest is usually the best.

In the 20th Century, the principle is seen when applied to good industrial design. The German designer Dieter Rams is considered one of the best. He summed up his life's work in his famous 10 principles of good design, the tenth of which is *Simplicity - as little design as possible - Less, but better – because it concentrates on the essential aspects, and the products are not burdened with non-essentials. Back to purity, back to simplicity.*

11

Rams' influence is seen in the work of Jonathan Ives at Apple whose design for the iPhone, iTouch and iPod are considered to be design classics. Their functionality and simplicity have captivated millions of loyal users. Simple, functional design that is perfectly adapted to its human user, in contrast to more complicated devices on the market at the time that forced the user to adapt to the machine.

In general terms, overly specialised systems are ultimately self-defeating because they impose constraints on the user that reduces them to a human-machine hybrid that is obliged to follow rigid procedures. Such systems are doomed to eventual failure because people will seek an alternative that does not de-humanise them. People operate best in an environment that allows them to grow and be creative.

In Nature, species that become too specialised are prone to extinction, while other species with generalised abilities that allow them to adapt to many environments tend to do very well. *Homo sapiens* is a prime example.

Flightless birds made the trade-off that in environments with sufficient food and an absence of predators, it was more adaptive for survival to eat their fill and in the process become too heavy to fly than it was to eat sparingly and retain the ability to fly.

Flightless birds, like the Dodo, became specialised for life in one environment. In the Dodo's case, this was the island of Mauritius in the Indian Ocean. When a new predator arrived in the form of man, they were too specialised to survive. These relatives of the pigeon had grown enormous, standing nearly a meter tall and weighing around 20 kilograms, making them easy prey for hungry sailors tired of sea-going rations. They stood still and allowed themselves to be clubbed. The Dodo was too specialised for its continued survival, unlike the sleek and light weight pigeon from which they evolved whose simple and efficient form allows it to adapt to different habitats.

In the commercial world, organisations and people who become too specialised are likely to go out of business or find themselves unemployed as society gradually evolves and demand for their particular product or service falls away. As discussed in the previous chapter, it is wise to look for the macro-trends in society and to proactively position yourself with the right skills and resources to successful meet the future when it arrives.

Non-action here means not acting in ways that are contrary to the broad trends that you are observing, and staying in harmony with the evolutionary forces that are evolving your society. (32)

Subtle influence

Many of the troubles of the world are reactions to earlier provocations. People or groups seek revenge for injuries inflicted by others, and in doing so, set up conditions for the trouble to be perpetuated. There is no shortage of examples of this phenomenon in the world at every level of society from nation states all the way down to individuals. It is the *'eye for an eye'* principle that comes down to us from the Old Testament of the Bible. It is high time we transcended this way of dealing with conflict because it does nothing to resolve it, only to perpetuate it.

Yet many scorn the *'turn the other cheek'* approach as being too soft. If you let someone walk all over you, they will keep doing it and regard you with contempt for letting them.

Both positions are extreme. What is called for is to find the middle path in which further conflict is neutralised and everyone concerned retains their self-respect while engendering respect for each other.

The middle path in this situation is the way of *subtle influence* by choosing a course of non-action or minimal action that is designed to produce no further reactions.

Understand first that what you resist will persist. Your resistance gives the problem energy and longer life. Strategic non-action in the first instance is therefore to refrain from action long enough for the trouble to dissipate of its own accord.

If the situation is such that something *must* be done sooner than later, then a minimalist course of action that expresses concern rather than blame will usually avoid the other party reacting angrily. Empathy is the key. It will give you insight into the appropriate course of action.

We are all human beings after all; one spectacularly successful species. In a real sense we are all members of a very large family. Look at your antagonist and use empathy to see the world through their eyes. Resist the 'us and them' mind-set that likes to create enemies. Realise that you would probably think and act just like them if you were in their place. They are you and you are they.

Use empathy to build a bridge of understanding with people and allow it to be your guide to exerting subtle influence. When you are empathic, the people you encounter sense this understanding in your demeanour and will generally react favourably to it. This is a reciprocal effect. When a person sees that you have made the effort to understand them, they will be more likely to make a similar effort to understand you.

Just as large ships are steered with small rudders, when action is necessary, the most subtle effort will yield the most effective result - a result that will not bring a whole new set of problems. (43)

Strategic non-action

Knowledge and understanding can come from two sources; interacting directly with the world, or through the cultivation of intuition.

Arguably, the most valuable knowledge you can acquire comes through intuition and the practice of non-interference. Why? Because intuitive knowledge addresses a deeper level of awareness than that gained through action, since knowledge that comes through action is obscured by situation-specific reactions.

On the other hand, a person can spend many years interacting with the world yet come to understand little about the true nature of life, so blinded is he by events.

Strategic non-action cultivates exceptional awareness of the world at a deep level. This awareness can help you to align your inner self with the outer world, to come into harmony with it.

Intuition can be cultivated by building awareness that your microcosmic inner self is a small but perfectly formed representation of the outside world, the macrocosm. This is how you are connected to all things; in a sense you *are* all things. The felt awareness of this truth is the enlightenment that people on the spiritual path seek. You don't just think it, you *feel* that it is true, know it at a deep level.

Intuition is the bridge between the world of form and the formless realm of ideas that lies deep within you, and which is the source of all creativity.

The prerequisite for being more intuitive is being able to silence the incessant noise that fills your consciousness as you go about your busy life. To hear the still, small voice of intuition, you must create *heightened awareness without the mental chatter*. This is the essence of meditation practice. (47)

Truth in non-action

Truth in non-action recognises that you receive pure information from observing an environment that is not *reacting* to you in any way. If you strip away the layers of pre-conceived ideas about the world, you are not filtering the input from your senses through the lens of orthodoxy.

Conventional wisdom suggests that to be wise, we must add to our knowledge daily. Yet the path to knowledge is no guarantee of wisdom. You may only acquire a large catalogue of facts without a deeper understanding coupled with a degree of disillusionment. As Oscar Wilde famously observed *What is a cynic? A man who knows the price of everything and the value of nothing.*

A more certain path to wisdom, even enlightenment, lies in strategic non-action as a way of accessing the unvarnished truth that is out there, all around you. If you act less and less on the world in an effort to influence affairs to your advantage you will eventually arrive at the point where you are motionless, poised with full potential. From here, you have intuitive access to all knowledge.

In the workplace, or in social situations, strategic non-action will often give you clear insight into the nature of situations. Clearly though, there will be times when you are required to perform a role, or think and act from an established body of knowledge in order to get your work done. Most jobs are like this. Doing nothing will get you fired. This is clearly not a time for inaction.

There are other times though, like sitting quietly in Nature, in your sanctuary, or in a public place and there is nothing you need to say or do. Non-action in this setting is a way of acquiring a deeper experience of the world and insight into how it works.

Stepping outside of an orthodox mind-set can be difficult. *Orthodoxy* simply means *what is held to be right*. It is a set of beliefs that a society has declared to be correct and unquestionable. The matter is closed to any further debate.

Yet as we know, nothing in the world is permanent, everything changes, evolves over time. This is true of the social environment as well as the physical environment. What was true once may no longer be true several hundred years later. Consider how many orthodox beliefs from 500 years ago are now considered absurd, from using leeches to extract disease from the blood to a flat earth around which the whole universe revolves.

It takes courage to honestly question the orthodox beliefs of your society and to rid oneself of delusion. People have a lot of investment in those beliefs, and if you are perceived to be a threat to them, you will experience and escalating response intended to neutralise the threat. For example, Galileo found evidence for a heliocentric solar system and narrowly avoided being condemned to death for it by the Roman Inquisition in 1615. He was found to be *vehemently suspect of heresy*, forced to recant, and lived under house arrest until his death in 1642.

At face value, what is being suggested here would seem to be at odds with the scientific method that relies on empirical evidence. Intuition alone never impressed the editor of a scholarly journal as a reliable source of knowledge. Yet there is ample evidence that the truly great men and women of science use intuition as an integral part of their method. The scientist has an intuitively-derived idea that serves as the starting point for observation. They do the research and write up the results so that others can repeat and extend the research. Intuition can be a most valuable part of this process.

As Einstein said *imagination* is more important than knowledge. When the physicist Nils Bohr, a contemporary of Einstein said that everything we call real is made of things that cannot be regarded as real he was expressing the paradox that cannot be explained by the logical scientific mind, but which can be apprehended by the intuitive mind. The truth is not only strange but stranger than you can imagine.

On a personal note, I have worked with more than a few brilliant minds. The only one I would regard as an outright genius was a professor of software engineering who despite an illustrious career was a deceptively humble man who meditated for two every day and learned classical Greek so he could read from the original texts. He did not say much, but when he did talk, it was well worth listening to. After he died, his widow said meditation was when he had his most brilliant ideas, the ones that made the biggest difference and earned him fame. (48)

Being non-confrontational

Infants have not yet acquired the layers of social conditioning that adults wear like a mantle. They are in moment-by-moment touch with their original nature and the current reality of their world. Human infants express the true nature of what it is to be human.

If we adopt an infant-like mind-set in our adult lives, we refrain from a range of adult actions that inevitably leads to stress. For example being confrontational, duplicitous, competitive, a whole range of social dangers.

The world is not inclined to harm an infant. They are spontaneous, accepting, adaptable, non-judgmental. They do not put themselves in harm's way by scrambling for wealth and power over the corpses of their adversaries. When pushed they yield and the pushers are thrown off balance and it appears to the rest of the world as aggression which mobilises opinion against the aggressor.

An infant is at the beginning of its life. Everything lies ahead. There is tremendous potential in being in this state. As people grow older and the self-limiting beliefs accumulate, there is a tendency for one's potential to diminish. By the time some people reach middle age, their options have shrunk to serving out another 10 or 15 years in a job they do not much like, then retirement on a limited income, leading ultimately to infirmity and death. Gone are the dreams of an unlimited future as they wait fearfully for the inevitable. The problem is not outside, it lies in their thinking.

These limitations are self-imposed, a result of the limiting beliefs about oneself that build up over time from their life experiences. Believe that you are too old to change careers, learn a new skill and sure enough, you are.

It certainly does not need to be so. It is not uncommon to see people in their middle to old age embarking on new careers, or a life of travel, or service to the community. It is their child-like love of life and their refusal to accept their perceived limitations that allows them to do this.

Strategic non-action in this sense is about avoiding the easy way of life that leads to the diminishment of your energies over time. It means, somewhat paradoxically, that greater effort is required to maintain a child-like mind-set which keeps you young and brimming with potential well into your advancing years. (55)

Path of least resistance

There is often little to be gained by emulating a bull-dozer and meeting difficult situations head-on. It becomes a test of strength and bravado; who will win, who will lose? Creating winners and losers also creates trouble in the form of lingering resentment. It has as much to do with wanting others to perceive you as being strong and fearless than it does with finding a resolution to the problem.

It is better to look objectively at the situation and see where the area of greatest weakness lies. Focus your attention on this area. This is the place that will be most receptive to your efforts. When that issue has been resolved, shift your attention to the next weakest area. Do this progressively; avoiding direct confrontation with a more powerful adversary, and the problem will be solved cleanly and without consequences. This of course requires considerable patience.

In the same way that a river finds its way through a valley of boulders, work your way around areas of resistance, knowing that you will ultimately wear them down. Most people are too impatient to take the long view, preferring the course of action calculated to produce quick results.

So it is that a complex situation can be influenced and controlled with small, non-confrontational actions that do not produce counter-reactions. Why complicate situations with counter-reactions?

Acting in a calm, serious manner inspires trust in others which breaks down resistance. By acting with subtlety and restraint you do not interfere with the natural order inherent in the situation. You become part of the natural process that is moving the situation towards its own conclusion.

Another perspective on this aspect of strategic non-action is to realise that every big situation was once small when it was new. Trying to influence the big, mature situation should be avoided in favour of having recognised it when it was new and taken action to influence it then when it was at its most receptive. This idea will be expanded on in the next chapter.

So the wise person anticipates that which will become difficult while it is still easy. They do what will become big while it is still small.

Human relationships in all of their diverse complexity can be most influenced at the beginning. For example children are impressionable, but as they grow older, they become less so. When that person reaches the full maturity of old-age, their opinions are largely fixed. When would it be best to try to influence them?

By following this strategy, you are able to exercise considerable influence in the world without incurring counter-reactions. The strategy emulates the water that flows around obstacles and eventually wears them down. (63)

Recognising the beginning

As briefly discussed in the previous chapter, it is much easier to influence people and events when they are at the beginning. Everything in world, when it first comes into existence, is small and relatively easy to influence. As entities, they have very little momentum yet. The tallest Redwood begins as a tiny seedling, the tallest building begins with the foundations, the longest journey begins with a single step.

A wise person learns to recognize these proto-events in their world. They get a sense for where and how things originate. They are then able to take action to influence them appropriately. This action should be minimal in nature, only as much as is necessary and no more.

The principle at work here is to not do so much that you interfere with the natural progression of events, and not hold on so tight to something that it is difficult to release when it is time to release it.

At university, for example, it is possible to influence people to think and act in appropriate ways for the profession they plan to enter. University students are generally young, or if more mature, understand that they need to be open to new information. Embodied in each student is a potential career spanning decades.

After several years, then decades of professional practice though, their habitual ways of doing their job becomes established, then entrenched. If the standards and practices of the profession changes during that time, which it inevitably will, the person finds that they are being left behind.

For those set in their ways, it is too late. Without a willingness to change, they will be marginalised or forced to retire. While they are still at university however, it can be impressed upon them that to succeed long-term in their career, they will need to be fully open to change; indeed to show leadership by being the proactive agent of change.

To successfully perform this aspect of strategic non-action, it is necessary to avoid the blind adoption of orthodox thinking that stifles innovation, at least as far as recognizing that no one way of doing something will last forever. Evolutionary change is necessary and inevitable.

A civil engineer, for example, when designing a suspension bridge will follow an established process model that has been developed over time, beginning as far back as the Industrial Revolution in the 19th century and which is accepted by the profession as being safe and effective. The beginning engineer is expected to follow the process model and not deviate from it. But if that engineer after having built 10 bridges can see an improved way of performing the process, one that better meets the needs of society for Sustainability for example, then he or she should propose this in professional forums and champion it. If the change is a good idea whose time has come, it will be incorporated into the process model for building suspension bridges and be part of the evolutionary change in the profession as it keeps pace with the needs of society. (64)

Give me freedom or give me death

The overwhelming majority of people in the world are inherently good-hearted and well-intentioned*. But only if they have personal freedom, intellectual independence, and most importantly, a life that is free from interference from authority.

So strong is people's need for freedom, that in the face tyranny, they are often willing to die in order to shake off the yoke and be free. This is how precious freedom is in the hearts of people. We see it clearly in the cases of various political revolutions, such as those in France, Russia, America and elsewhere. In every case the revolution happened because people found their rulers intolerable.

The message is clear to managers and leaders of all kinds, including parents. If they are not to rebel, even to their own detriment, the people over whom you exercise control *must* be given sufficient room and resources to enable them to reach their full potential, to self-actualize. It is a very deeply felt need, expressed as the need for freedom.

As a leader, you should refrain from imposing *unnecessary* rules and restrictions on people (or on yourself). A well-regulated society needs normative rules, but people also need to see the need for those rules, how they operate for the benefit of all. They should have some say in the formulation of these rules.

---

* Excluding the 1 to 3% of society who display psychopathic tendencies (see Appendix for how to recognize a psychopath).

The element of strategic non-action therefore focuses on refraining from excessive action that interferes with people's freedom and generates simmering resentment.

One source of excessive rules is the application of military-style discipline to children or employees on the assumption that if it works in the military it should work elsewhere, or perhaps the leader believes that war is not far away, and the children need to be toughened up. Unfortunately for all concerned, this rarely results in good outcomes.

In the military, it is necessary that soldiers be trained to follow orders even under the most extreme circumstances. This really does require a lot of discipline and well-trained soldiers come to understand the need for discipline and to take a certain pride in having achieved it. In families or organisations however, the same imperative does not exist, and the discipline quickly comes to be seen as unnecessary and oppressive.

Oppressive leaders always end up being hurt by their own actions, either directly by people's reactions or indirectly through the people in their environment mobilising against them in some way.

An oppressive leader believes their personal interests are identical to the interests of the group (or organisation). They see themselves as the embodiment of the group. It can lead them to indulge in self-gratifying pursuits that are not in the best interests of the group. Feeling somewhat guilty perhaps, the oppressive leader reacts by unjustly curtailing the freedom of the people even further. There is no shortage of examples of this kind of indulgent, often extravagant behavior in despotic leaders. It is an illustration of Lord

Acton's famous quote that *power tends to corrupt, and absolute power corrupts absolutely. Great men are almost always bad men.*

As the regime becomes more oppressive, the people's suffering increases. Perhaps they have to work long hours in poor conditions. Maybe they do not get enough to eat, or disease goes untreated. All the while contempt for the leader grows. There can be only one outcome – the leader's eventual demise.

So the enlightened leader refrains from limiting people's freedom. Instead they behave unselfishly and provide people with the means to grow and fulfil their potential. The leader gives them the space in which to express that potential, then they stand back and leave them to it. This is enlightened non-action (74 & 75)

Conclusion

To become a master of strategic non-action, cultivate and practice these principles:

- Limit your impact on the world to avoid creating counter-reactions that become problems in their own right.

- Allow a clear flow of information to enter your senses from a world that is not busy reacting to you. This leads to a deeper, intuitive awareness of reality.

- Further improve the flow of clear information by shedding orthodox ideas that stifle new ways of thinking.

- Acknowledge that problems have a way of resolving themselves in time and that action should be limited to guiding the situation to resolve itself.

- Adopt a humble posture and allow natural forces to advance you, knowing that what was low becomes high, what was in the background comes to the foreground.

- Recognize and respect that there is an inner pattern, an *Informing Principle* in Nature. Align your awareness with this principle and you will be in harmony with Nature.

- Being adaptable in a changing world is about not becoming too specialised, too dependent on a specific set of circumstances for your survival. Simplicity is the key.

- Understand that what you resist will persist. By paying attention to a problem, you strengthen it. Some problems are best left alone to fade away.

- Avoid the extremes of seeking revenge on the one hand and being a door-mat on the other. Find the middle path by choosing a course of strategic minimal action that neutralises conflict and produces no further reactions.

- Emulate a child; live in the Now, be adaptable, non-judgmental, stay in touch with your original nature and the reality of your world as it is, not as you believe it should be.

- Avoid meeting tough problems head-on; solve them progressively by focussing on the weakest aspect first, then the next and the next. Be like the stream that flows around obstacles on its way to its goal.

- Understand that it is much easier to influence people and events when they are at the beginning.

- Be the kind of leader that gives people the resources they need to grow, the space in which to grow, and then step back and leave to get on with it. Respect their need for freedom and self-determination by not imposing unnecessary rules.

- Learn *patience* in all things; it is rightly said that patience is the paramount virtue.

The End

Appendix:
How to recognize a psychopath

Psychopaths (or people suffering from Antisocial Personality Disorder as it is correctly called) have been described as "intra-species predators" or predators who prey on members of their own species. On average it affects around 3% of males, and 1% of females. In an evolutionary sense, they are confidence tricksters who make their living by parasitizing the remaining 98% of the population.

Robert Hare's Psychopathy Checklist is a commonly used diagnostic tool. It is presented here (with thanks to the author) as a guide only. Consult a registered Psychologist or Psychiatrist for definitive advice on this matter.

Personality Factors

- Glibness/superficial charm
- Grandiose sense of self-worth
- Pathological lying
- Cunning/manipulative
- Lack of remorse or guilt
- Shallow affect (genuine emotion is short-lived and egocentric)
- Callousness; lack of empathy
- Failure to accept responsibility for own actions

Behavioral Factors

- Need for stimulation/proneness to boredom
- Parasitic lifestyle
- Poor behavioral control
- Lack of realistic long-term goals
- Impulsivity
- Irresponsibility
- Juvenile delinquency
- Early behavior problems

Traits not correlated with either factor

- Promiscuous sexual behavior
- Many short-term marital relationships
- Criminal versatility

CPSIA information can be obtained
at www.ICGtesting.com
Printed in the USA
LVOW13s1810311017
554459LV00025B/337/P

9 781467 928533